Shanyi Goes to China

For Helena, Natascha, Ivy, Derek, Ming and Sebastian

First published in Great Britain and the USA in 2006 by
Frances Lincoln Children's Books, 4 Torriano Mews,
Torriano Avenue, London NW5 2RZ
www.franceslincoln.com

Distributed in the USA by Publishers Group West

British Library Cataloguing in Publication Data
available on request

ISBN 10: 1-84507-470-X
ISBN 13: 978-1-84507-470-8

Printed in Singapore

1 3 5 7 9 8 6 4 2

Shanyi Goes
to China

Sungwan So

F

FRANCES LINCOLN
CHILDREN'S BOOKS

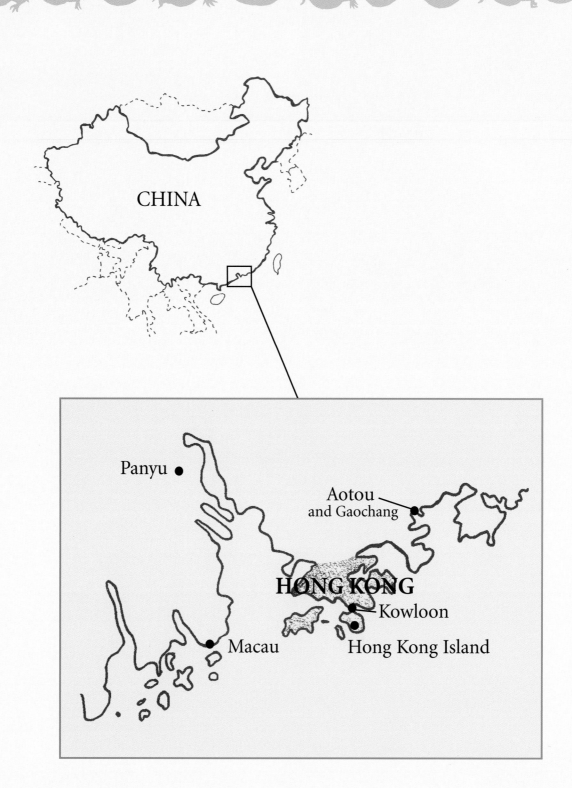

CHINA

Panyu •

Aotou
and Gaochang •

HONG KONG

Macau •

Kowloon

Hong Kong Island

I'm Ivy So. I have a Chinese name too. It's Sinyin in Cantonese and Shanyi in Mandarin. It means "kindhearted and cheerful" – and I am!

I'm very excited. My little brother Derek and I are going to China with Mum and Dad to see where they were born!

I was only three years old when I last went to China, and I don't remember much about that trip. This time I'm going to write everything down so that I can share it with my friends when I get back.

Hong Kong

We arrived late at Hong Kong International Airport
and stayed with Uncle Wong overnight. Mum said,
"Get a good sleep, because we're going to be very busy!"

Panyu

Today we took the train and bus with Popo (Mum's mother) to Panyu, where Taipo (my great-grandma) lives. Taipo gave us *hongbao*, red envelopes filled with Chinese money.

Panyu

This morning, when we went out, Dad said, "They say that China is the kingdom of bicycles." I looked around and said, "But it's the land of motorcycles now!"

Popo took us to the Panyu Xingjian Safari Park. About half of the white tigers in the world live here.

I was so happy when I saw the giant panda Dongdong – she looked soft and furry. I said to Dad, "Please, please take some good pictures of Dongdong and me together". So he did.

Great-uncle Yaoliang invited us to dinner. On his kitchen table there was an altar to the Zaoshen (kitchen god) who looks after families. We each had our own bowl of rice and shared dishes from the middle of the table.

Panyu

Today, Great-uncle Yaolin took us to see a new school paid for by Chinese people living overseas. Derek played outside with one of the two stone lions guarding the school.

Then we went to see Baomo yuan, a traditional Chinese garden. I've never seen so many fish! When we dropped food in the ponds, hundreds of carp jumped up with their mouths wide open.

Aotou

Today we went to the seaside! Aotou is where Uncle Sungtak lives. Yeye (Dad's father) and Nainai (Dad's mother) were staying at Uncle Sungtak's house too. Aotou smelled of the sea and salted fish.

Uncle Sungtak kept thirty chickens in big cages behind the kitchen. I felt a bit sorry for them and helped to feed them.

Yeye told us that his grandfather once had a shop on the pier. He used to buy fish from the fishermen and lend them fishing nets, in the days when fishermen were not allowed to live on land.

In the afternoon lots of small fishing boats came into the wharf. Families repaired their fishing nets and sold fish and seafood – crabs, shrimps, clams and oysters.

Gaochang

Yeye was very excited, because we were going to visit our ancestral hall in Gaochong village. Inside the hall Yeye lit candles and showed us a red wooden memorial tablet with our family name carved on it.

Nainai and Uncle Sungtak prepared offerings of food and wine, and I helped to put incense on the Tudi (a local god of the land). Then we all stepped up, bowed and offered incense to our ancestors.

The best bit was when we helped Nainai burn money for our ancestors' ghosts to spend in the afterlife!

Today we said goodbye to Uncle Sungtak. Yeye and Nainai wanted to show us Macau, where they live. As we went past Hong Kong Island on the ferry, I could see hundreds of skyscrapers.

Yeye took us downtown to see the city. Macau looks different from other Chinese places. It was once a Portuguese colony and has Portuguese buildings and churches.

Everyone was out shopping, and Mum bought
me a wonderful New Year outfit. Nainai said,
"You look lovely – just like a real Chinese girl."

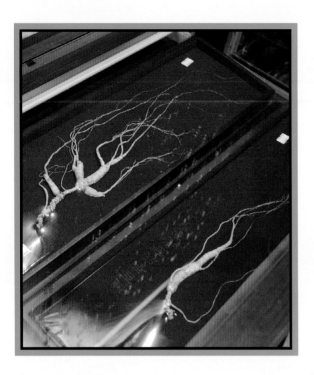

Uncle Albert, Dad and Mum's schoolfriend from America took us to a pharmacy selling herbs and ginseng – a very special Chinese medicine.

Suddenly Dad said, "Look!" He'd spotted lots of old things for sale on the ground – jade, crosses, a sword and even a statue of Mao, who used to be the Chinese Communist leader.

We dragged Dad away and into a garden where musicians were practising Cantonese songs with traditional two-stringed Chinese instruments called *erhu*. Then we went back to Yeye and Nainai's home.

This morning, Nainai took us to the temple where
Great-grandma's ashes are kept. She showed us statues
of Guanyin, "the Goddess who looks down on the World".
The statue inside, "Guanyin-with-a-thousand-arms",
is very special, reaching out to people who need help.

The last Guanyin we saw was standing on the seashore. She was standing on a lotus base which had a whole exhibition centre inside.

"Would you like *dim sum* for lunch?" Nainai asked. We said yes, and it turned out to be lots of food in little bamboo baskets. Afterwards we were too full to do anything else!

Macau

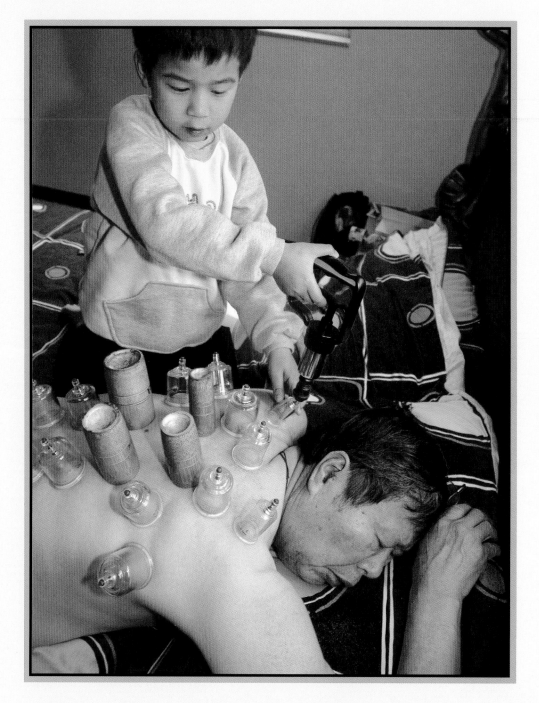

Today Dad gave Yeye a foot massage and Derek
helped to do cupping – a Chinese way of helping
the blood go round the body. We used two types
of cups – bamboo and modern plastic ones.

Nainai went off to the local market to buy food for lunch
and when she came back, she cooked us steamed egg custard.

Yeye showed us how to
write our names in beautiful
Chinese writing called
calligraphy. Then it was
time to catch the ferry to
Hong Kong Island, to stay
with Mum's friend, Uncle Li.

Hong Kong Island

A whole day on Hong Kong Island! We went in a slow double-decker tram through the old part to the new district. Then we took a tram up Victoria Peak.

What a fantastic view there is, looking down on both sides of Victoria Harbour! The high-rise buildings seemed tiny.

Popo and Gong-gong (Mum's father) took us out to dinner. While we were waiting for the other guests we watched them playing a special Chinese board game called *mahjong*.

Kowloon

Today we went to Kowloon, across the Harbour from Hong Kong Island. When we got there, we went to see a wooden Buddhist temple called Chi Lin Nunnery. Dad said it had been built without a single nail. He was right! I looked and looked, but I couldn't see one anywhere.

Then we took the underground train to Mongkok and went shopping. Dad thought he was going down with a cold, and bought some Chinese herbal medicine to stop it getting worse.

Last of all, Popo took us on a fast ride up a 66-storey building. I felt a bit dizzy at the top, but it was exciting.

Hong Kong Island

Our last day in China! We shared a goodbye meal with Dad's best friends and their families.

On the way to the airport, Dad showed me Ching Ma Bridge, the world's biggest road-and-rail suspension bridge. But I was thinking about my big family in China – I didn't want to say goodbye to them.

Now my journal is full up! Just one more thing: one day, I want to go back to China.

Steamed Egg Custard
cooked for Shanyi

Serves 4

You'll need:

◆ 6 eggs

◆ 120g (½ cup) sugar

◆ 250ml (1 cup) milk

◆ 350ml (1½ cups) water

✛ a grown-up on hand to help you.

1. Heat the water in a saucepan, add the sugar and stir until the sugar totally dissolves. Let the water cool down to room temperature.

2. Whisk the eggs in a big bowl.

3. Add the milk and the cooled-down sugar-water to the eggs, and stir well.

4. Pour the mixture into small bowls and cover the tops tightly with aluminium foil.

5. Bring water to the boil in a steamer and put the small bowls into the steamer – they should not touch the water underneath. Steam for 8-10 minutes and serve.

Glossary

afterlife: life after death. Many Chinese believe that their spirits will join their ancestors after they die.

ancestral hall: hall built for family ceremonies.

Buddhist: a person who follows Buddha. Buddhists believe that desires cause suffering, and that trying to live wisely and meditating will release them from desire, suffering and rebirth.

calligraphy: the art of fine handwriting.

Cantonese: the people and the dialect spoken in Guangzhou province, in Southern China.

carp: a beautiful freshwater fish often bred in ponds and lakes.

cupping: traditional Chinese medical treatment. Cups are applied to the skin to suck out any substances blocking the body's energy and blood flow.

dim sum: traditional Cantonese cuisine in which small portions of steamed, fried, salted or sweet foods are served one after another.

erhu: traditional two-stringed instrument played with a bow.

ginseng: rare plant with forked roots used as herbal medicine.

Guanyin: a goddess in the Buddhist religion.

hongbao: small red envelope with money inside given as a blessing.

jade: pale green or white mineral used to make gemstones or carvings.

lotus: water plant with large leaves and sweet-smelling pinkish flowers, symbolising purity in Buddhism.

mahjong: Chinese board game for four players.

Mandarin: the official language spoken in China.

Mao: Mao Zedong, founder of the People's Republic of China.

Tudi: an important deity in Chinese folk religion, a local god of the land or village. He is usually portrayed as a very old man living beneath the earth.

Zaoshen: important deity in Chinese folk religion. He watches over each family by their kitchen stove and reports to the God of Heaven at the end of the year.

Index

前坡壁賦典
淡珍

辛巳冬
慶彬書